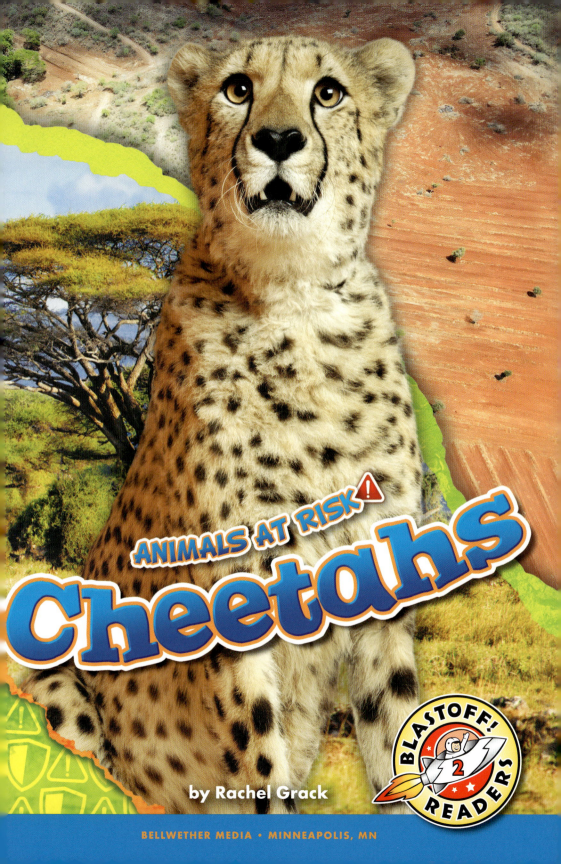

Blastoff! Readers are carefully developed by literacy experts to build reading stamina and move students toward fluency by combining standards-based content with developmentally appropriate text.

Level 1 provides the most support through repetition of high-frequency words, light text, predictable sentence patterns, and strong visual support.

Level 2 offers early readers a bit more challenge through varied sentences, increased text load, and text-supportive special features.

Level 3 advances early-fluent readers toward fluency through increased text load, less reliance on photos, advancing concepts, longer sentences, and more complex special features.

★ **Blastoff! Universe**

This edition first published in 2023 by Bellwether Media, Inc.

No part of this publication may be reproduced in whole or in part without written permission of the publisher. For information regarding permission, write to Bellwether Media, Inc., Attention: Permissions Department, 6012 Blue Circle Drive, Minnetonka, MN 55343.

Library of Congress Cataloging-in-Publication Data

Names: Koestler-Grack, Rachel A., 1973- author.
Title: Cheetahs / by Rachel Grack.
Description: Minneapolis, MN : Bellwether Media, 2023. | Series: Blastoff! readers: animals at risk | Includes bibliographical references and index. | Audience: Ages 5-8 | Audience: Grades 2-3 | Summary: "Relevant images match informative text in this introduction to cheetahs. Intended for students in kindergarten through third grade"-- Provided by publisher.
Identifiers: LCCN 2022000419 (print) | LCCN 2022000420 (ebook) | ISBN 9781644877111 (library binding) | ISBN 9781648347573 (ebook)
Subjects: LCSH: Cheetah--Juvenile literature. | Cheetah--Conservation--Juvenile literature.
Classification: LCC QL737.C23 K635 2023 (print) | LCC QL737.C23 (ebook) | DDC 599.75/9--dc23/eng/20220113
LC record available at https://lccn.loc.gov/2022000419
LC ebook record available at https://lccn.loc.gov/2022000420

Text copyright © 2023 by Bellwether Media, Inc. BLASTOFF! READERS and associated logos are trademarks and/or registered trademarks of Bellwether Media, Inc.

Editor: Kieran Downs   Designer: Brittany McIntosh

Printed in the United States of America, North Mankato, MN.

Table of Contents

Fast Cats	4
In Danger!	8
Save the Cheetahs!	12
Glossary	22
To Learn More	23
Index	24

Fast Cats

Cheetahs are long, thin wild cats with spotted **coats**. They are the fastest animals on land!

Five **subspecies** live in parts of Africa and Iran.

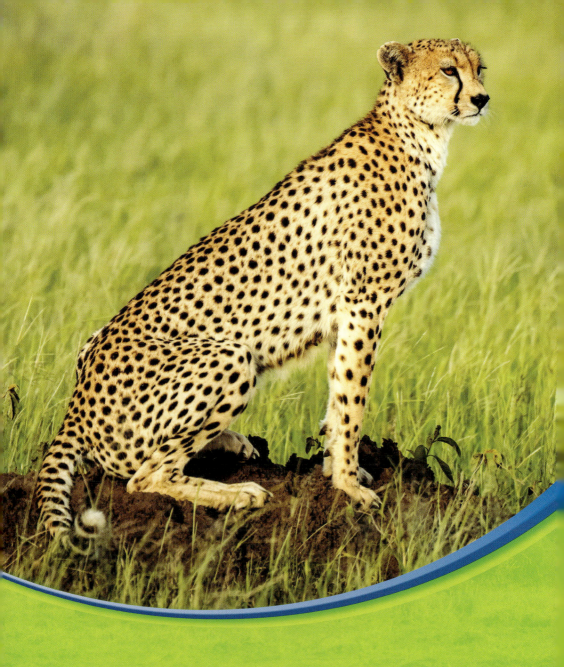

Cheetahs once had large **home ranges**. But people spread into their **habitats**.

Many cheetahs died. They still face big troubles today.

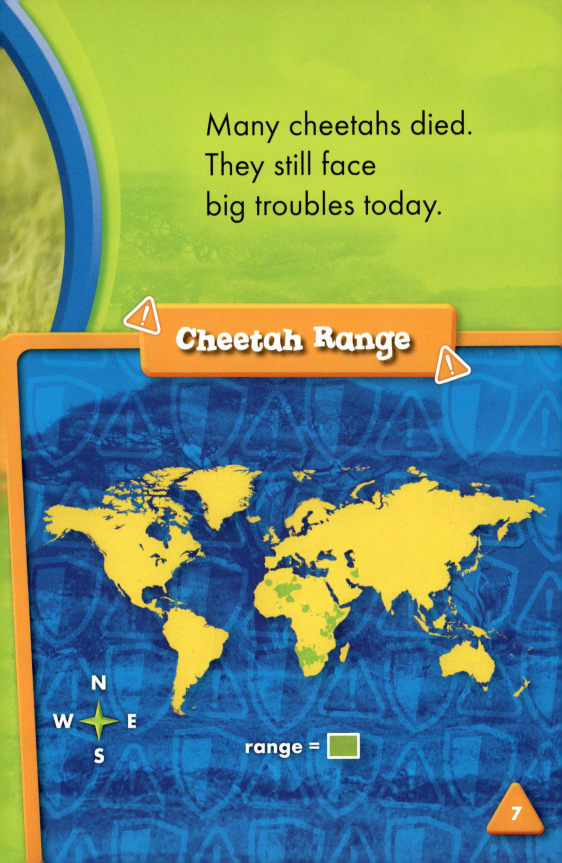

Cheetah Range

range =

In Danger!

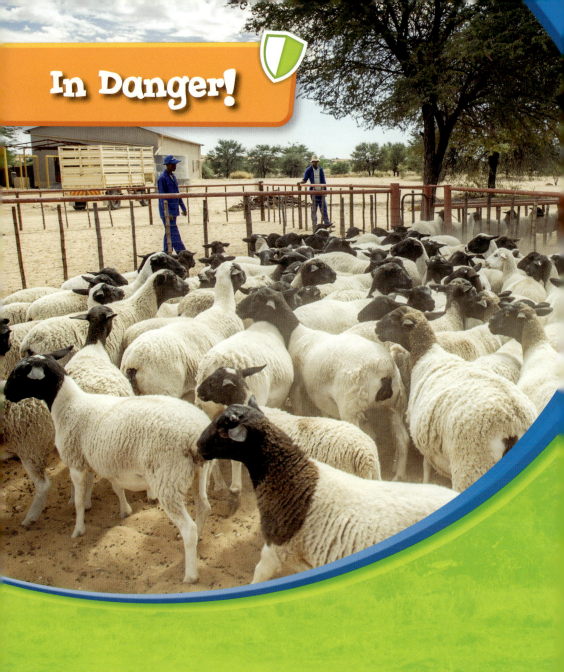

Cheetahs hunt on open **savannas**. But people clear this land for farms and towns.

Antelopes and gazelles have nowhere to **graze**. Cheetahs lose their main **prey**.

Threats

1. people clear savannas

2. people make farmland

3. cheetahs lose habitat and food

Hungry cheetahs may hunt **livestock**. Farmers shoot them to save their animals.

Climate change hurts cheetahs, too. It makes their homes too hot.

livestock

Cheetah Stats

conservation status: vulnerable

life span: about 12 years

Save the Cheetahs!

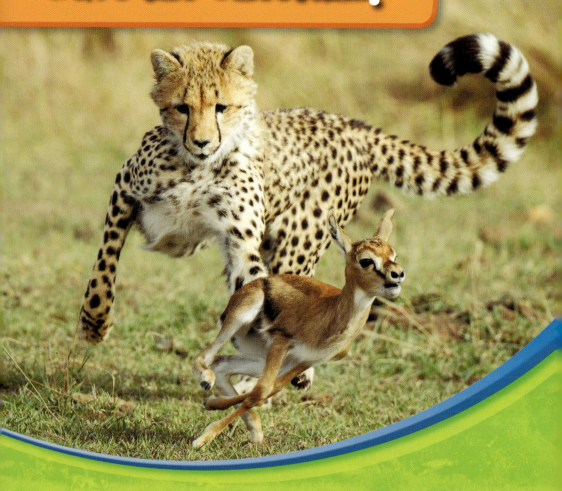

Cheetahs keep savanna **ecosystems** healthy. Without them, antelope and gazelle **herds** would grow too big.

Cheetahs may leave food for other animals, too.

The World with Cheetahs

1. more cheetahs

2. healthy antelope and gazelle herds

3. healthy savannas

Governments in Africa set aside land for cheetahs.

Some zoos help cheetahs **breed** healthy cubs. One day, more cheetahs may live in the wild.

People teach farmers how to grow crops on less land.

Cheetah habitats can go untouched. Savannas may be even larger someday.

Wildlife workers give guard dogs to farmers. The dogs chase away cheetahs.

guard dog

Farmers do not have to hurt cheetahs. Both farm animals and cheetahs stay safe.

Everyone can help cheetahs. Riding bikes instead of driving places helps slow climate change.

People can **donate** money, too. There are many ways to save these beautiful cats!

Glossary

breed—to produce young

climate change—a human-caused change in Earth's weather due to warming temperatures

coats—the hair or fur covering some animals

donate—to give gifts for a certain cause; most people donate money.

ecosystems—communities of plants and animals living in certain places

graze—to feed on growing plants

habitats—places and natural surroundings in which plants or animals live

herds—groups of animals that live and travel together

home ranges—the lands on which groups of animals live and travel

livestock—animals raised on a farm, such as goats, sheep, and cows

prey—animals that are hunted by other animals for food

savannas—flat grasslands with few trees

subspecies—different kinds of one type of animal

To Learn More

AT THE LIBRARY
Amstutz, Lisa J. *A Day in the Life of a Cheetah: A 4D Book*. North Mankato, Minn.: Pebble, 2019.

Emminizer, Theresa. *Speedy Cheetahs*. New York, N.Y.: PowerKids Press, 2021.

Rossiter, Brienna. *Saving Earth's Animals*. Lake Elmo, Minn.: Focus Readers, 2022.

ON THE WEB

FACTSURFER

Factsurfer.com gives you a safe, fun way to find more information.

1. Go to www.factsurfer.com.

2. Enter "cheetahs" into the search box and click 🔍.

3. Select your book cover to see a list of related content.

Index

Africa, 5, 14
antelopes, 9, 12
breed, 15
climate change, 10, 20
coats, 4
cubs, 15
donate, 20
ecosystems, 12
farms, 8, 10, 16, 18, 19
food, 13
gazelles, 9, 12
governments, 14
guard dogs, 18
habitats, 6, 17
home ranges, 6
hunt, 8, 10
Iran, 5
livestock, 10
people, 6, 8, 16, 20

prey, 9
range, 7
savannas, 8, 12, 17
stats, 11
subspecies, 5
threats, 9
towns, 8
ways to help, 20
wild cats, 4, 20
wildlife workers, 18
world with, 13
zoos, 15

The images in this book are reproduced through the courtesy of: Eric Isselee, front cover, pp. 3, 22; Noor Santosian, front cover (back top), pp. 3, 9 (top right), 23; PHOTOCREO Michal Bednarek, front cover (back bottom); Stu Porter, pp. 4, 12; Thorsten Spoerlein, p. 5; Design Pics Inc/ Alamy Stock Photo, p. 6; Edwin Remsberg/ Alamy-Stock Photo, pp. 8, 9 (top left); Thomas Retterath, p. 9 (bottom); 1001slide, p. 10; Vaganundo_Che, pp. 10-11; AfricaWildlife, p. 13 (top left); MishaelK, p. 13 (top right); TTphoto, p. 13 (bottom); Welshboy2020, p. 14; REUTERS/ Alamy Stock Photo, p. 15; Edwin Remsberg/ Alamy Stock Photo, p. 16; Wirestock Creators, p. 17; Bobby Bradley, p. 18; Michal Ninger, p. 19; Jacek Chabraszewski, p. 20; GUDKOV ANDREY, pp. 20-21.